T4-ABL-885

Building ON A Dream

Fallingwater

Tamra B. Orr

PURPLE TOAD
PUBLISHING

PURPLE TOAD PUBLISHING

Copyright © 2019 by Purple Toad Publishing, Inc. All rights reserved. No part of this book may be reproduced without written permission from the publisher. Printed and bound in the United States of America.

Printing 1 2 3 4 5 6 7 8 9

BUILDING ON A DREAM

Big Ben
The Burj Khalifa
The Eiffel Tower
The Empire State Building
Fallingwater
The Flatiron Building
The Golden Gate Bridge
The Great Wall of China
The International Space Station
The Leaning Tower of Pisa
The Louvre
The Space Needle
The Statue of Liberty
The Sydney Opera House
The Taj Mahal
The Trevi Fountain
The White House

Library of Congress Cataloging-in-Publication Data
Orr, Tamara, B.
   Building on a Dream: Fallingwater / Written by Tamara B. Orr.
      p. cm.
Includes bibliographical references, glossary and index.
ISBN 9781624694332
1. Frank Lloyd Wright 1867-1959 — Juvenile Literature. 2. — American Architects — Fallingwater, Pennsylvania — Juvenile Literature. 3. Kauffman Family — Homes — Fallingwater — Juvenile Literature. I. Series: Building on a Dream: Fallingwater
  NA737.W7 2019
  728/.372/092
                                                                            Library of Congress Control Number: 2018944209
eBook ISBN: 9781624694325

ABOUT THE AUTHOR: Tamra B. Orr is a full-time author who lives in the Pacific Northwest. She has written more than 500 educational books for readers of all ages. A graduate of Ball State University in Muncie, Indiana, Orr and her family enjoy camping in tents under the stars. She lives 20 minutes away from the beautiful Multnomah Falls and dreams of having a house close enough to hear them.

CONTENTS

Chapter One
An Argument 5

Chapter Two
The Architect and the Homeowner 9

Chapter Three
In Harmony with Nature 13

Chapter Four
Welcome to the Cave 17

Chapter Five
A Few Flaws 23

Chronology 26

Chapter Notes 28

Further Reading 29

Books 29

Works Consulted 29

On the Internet 30

Glossary 31

Index 32

Cantilevers are supports that are anchored on one end (see diagram, left). They are often used in bridges, such as in the Whirlpool Rapids Bridge at Niagara Falls (above). Frank Lloyd Wright (center) wanted to use cantilevers to support the terraces at Fallingwater.

CHAPTER 1

An Argument

He said. . . . He said.

It was an argument that would ripple through decades.

Frank Lloyd Wright was considered one of the best architects in the world—and he agreed completely. He once told reporter Mike Wallace, "I've been accused of saying I was the greatest architect in the world and if I had said so, I don't think it would be very arrogant, because I don't believe there are many [great architects]—if any."[1]

The homeowner was Edgar J. Kaufmann Sr. He was rich, powerful, and, at the moment, worried. He had chosen Wright to design his summer home. He loved the architect's plans for a house with huge terraces straddling a waterfall. Kaufmann deeply respected Wright's talent. But there was a problem. Walter Hall, the engineer who was on the building site every day, did not think those terraces had enough support under them. Even with the cantilevers holding them up, he was afraid the house's heavy concrete and rock floors would sag. Then, after enough years, they would collapse into the waterfall below.

Understandably concerned, Kaufmann asked a contracting company to conduct tests on the cantilevers. Were they safe? The contractors agreed with the engineer. More steel supports were needed.

When Wright found out about this, he was furious. His designs were being questioned? How dare they! He immediately wrote a letter to Kaufmann. It read,

Chapter 1

My dear E.J.,
If you are paying to have the concrete engineering done down there, there is no use whatever in our doing it here. I am willing you should take it over but I am not willing to be insulted. . . . I don't know what kind of architect you are familiar with, but

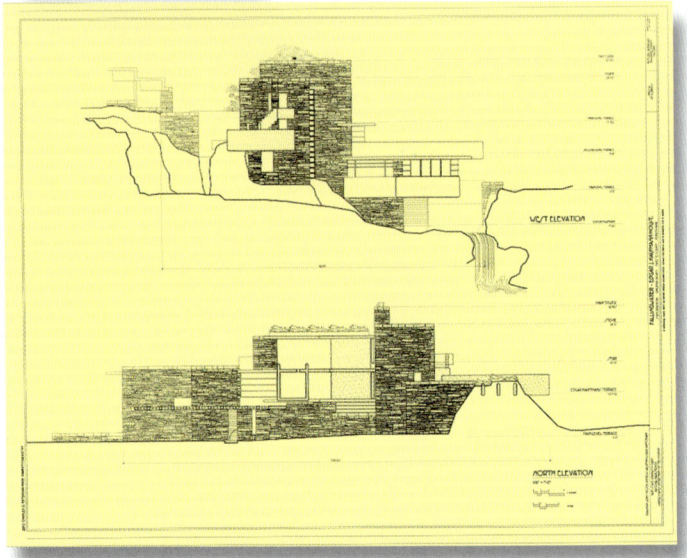

Plans for the outside of Fallingwater show how it nestles into the hillside.

it apparently isn't the kind I think I am. You seem not to know how to treat a decent one. I have put so much more into this house than you or any other client has a right to expect that if I haven't your confidence—to hell with the whole thing.

Sincerely yours, Frank Lloyd Wright, Architect[2]

Kaufmann was a wise and experienced businessman. He knew he had to handle this angry architect carefully. In return, he wrote,

Dear Mr. Wright,
If you have been paid to do the concrete engineering up there, there is no use whatever of our doing it down here. I am not willing to take it over as you suggest, nor am I willing to be insulted. . . . I don't know what kind of clients you are familiar with, but apparently they are not the kind I think I am. You seem not to know how to treat a decent one. I have put so much confidence and enthusiasm

An Argument

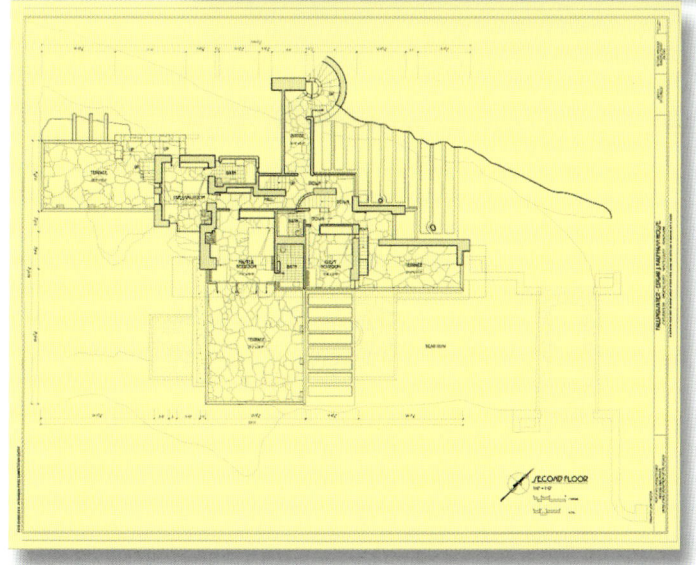

According to legend, it took only two hours to draw the floor plan.

behind this whole project in my limited way, to help the fulfillment of your efforts that if I do not have your confidence in the matter . . . to hell with the whole thing.

Sincerely yours, Edgar J. Kaufmann

P.S. Now don't you think that we should stop writing letters and that you owe it to the situation to come to Pittsburgh and clear it up by getting the facts?[3]

In the end, Hall made the decision. Without telling Wright, he doubled the steel used in the original plans and added a supporting wall. It was a wise decision. Had Hall not done so, Fallingwater, the house known as one of Wright's masterpieces, would have slowly sunk into the roaring waters below (risking a new nickname of Falling IN Water). Even doubled, the supports for this unusual project would prove to be too weak. The thousands of dollars spent building the house would be nothing compared to the millions it would take to update and repair it years later.

Fallingwater Facts	
Years of construction	1936–1938
Interior (square feet)	2,885
Terraces (square feet)	2,445
Guest house square footage	1,700
Final cost	$155,000
Visitors since 1964 (2017)	5.5 million

The Carnegie Science Center in Pittsburgh displays a model of Fallingwater in its Miniature Railroad & Village. The site for the home is just over an hour's drive from Pittsburgh.

CHAPTER 2

The Architect and the Homeowner

Fallingwater is one of the most unusual and beautiful homes in the United States. It was built in the forests of southwestern Pennsylvania, about 65 miles from Pittsburgh. Every year, people travel from all over the world to tour it. Built more than eighty years ago, Fallingwater is a glimpse into the past, just before the beginning of World War II. The home still has most of its original furnishings, including artwork and statues.

There were two men behind this masterpiece. The first was architect Frank Lloyd Wright. The second was department store owner Edgar Kaufmann Sr. The two of them usually got along well and had high respect for each other.

Frank Lloyd Wright was born in 1867 in Wisconsin. From the time he was a small boy, he loved being outdoors and in nature. He was fascinated by the changing of the seasons and how it affected colors and shadows. He later remembered, "The modeling of the hills, the weaving and fabric that clings to them, the look of it all tender green or covered with snow or in full glow of summer that bursts into the glorious blaze of autumn . . . I still feel myself as much a part of it as the trees and the birds and bees are, and the red barns."[1] His passion for nature showed in almost every building he designed. Nowhere was this truer than at Fallingwater.

For many years, Wright's designs had gotten attention. He created plans for everything from homes to museums to office buildings. By the time he died in 1959, more than 500 of the 1,100 buildings he had

Chapter 2

designed had been built. His style was often called "organic." This meant that he tried to involve nature in his plans.

When Kaufmann met Wright in 1934 and asked him to design his summer home along Bear Run Tributary, the architect was well into his sixties. He had not designed a building since 1929. Many of the modern architects respected Wright's work, but felt it was outdated and old-fashioned. Driven to teach and share this knowledge about art, Wright wrote his autobiography. Then he created an art studio and school at one of his favorite boyhood spots in Wisconsin. It was called Taliesin, a Welsh word meaning "shining brow." He named it in honor

Taliesin was built specifically without gutters so that sparkling icicles would form.

The Architect and the Homeowner

of his Welsh grandparents. As Wright described it, "I turned to this hill in the Valley as my grandfather before me had turned to America—as a hope and haven."[2] From Taliesin, Wright taught young artists many topics, including construction, farming, gardening, cooking, music, and art. One of his young apprentices was Edgar Kauffman Jr. He came to the studio for six months. In the process, as some believe, he introduced the famous architect to his well-known father.

Among the artwork in Fallingwater is a portrait of Edgar J. Kaufmann Sr.

Edgar Kaufmann Sr., born in 1885, was a smart businessman. In addition to being the head of a chain of successful department stores, he was also known for supporting the arts and culture in his community. He was handsome, charming, and wealthy, even though the rest of the country was in the midst of the Great Depression. For most people, jobs were scarce. What money was available was used to pay for necessities such as food and rent. Having enough spare money to build a new house was rare. Kaufmann was one of those rarities.

Kaufmann had a small summer home at Bear Run. He often used it with his wife and son, or to host some of his many employees. Once he met Wright, however, he had a completely new idea for the cabin. He wanted to replace it with a beautiful home across from the stunning waterfalls. Who better to do that than the man who always put nature first in his designs?

Fallingwater is located in Pennsylvania's Laurel Highlands. The hike from the Visitors Center to the house is a quarter mile. Visitors can request a ride to the house on a shuttle bus, but these are limited.

CHAPTER 3

In Harmony with Nature

Look around your house. Does it have a theme? Do all the pieces fit together as one?

If Frank Lloyd Wright had designed it, it probably would. He strongly felt that all architecture should merge together. It should be in harmony. "In organic architecture then, it is quite impossible to consider the building as one thing, its furnishings another and its setting and environment still another," he stated. "The spirit in which these buildings are conceived sees all these together at work as *one thing*."[1] When Wright designed a building, he often continued his plans to include what furniture, rugs, lighting, dishes, and glass should be used.

This was true with Fallingwater. When Wright came out to see the property for the first time in 1934, he was astounded at the beauty of the area. The site was in the middle of lush green trees, with a bubbling stream and a waterfall. He heard the rushing water, smelled the green trees, and saw the colorful flash of birds and wildflowers in the forest. He was eager to build a special house there. He pictured the home like a protective cave in the middle of nature.

In an interview with Hugh Downs in 1954, Wright recalled the impact of the site. "There in a beautiful forest was a solid, high rock ledge rising beside a waterfall, and the natural thing seemed to be to cantilever the house from that rock bank over the falling water. Then came (of course) Mr. Kaufmann's love for the beautiful site," he continued. "He loved the site where the house was built and liked to

Chapter 3

listen to the waterfall. So that was a prime motive in the design. I think that you can hear the waterfall when you look at the design. At least it is there, and he lives intimately with the thing he loves."[2]

After visiting the site, Wright thought a great deal about what he should do with it. Months passed. Kaufmann grew more and more eager to see the plans for his new summer home. Legend has it that, one afternoon, he called the architect and said he would be coming by in a couple of hours to see the blueprints. There was only one problem: Wright had not actually drawn any plans yet.

Wright also had a passion for expensive and exotic cars, which he described as "architecture on wheels."

Edgar Taffel, one of Wright's apprentices at the time, was there when that phone call came in. He described the moment in his book *Years with Frank Lloyd Wright: Apprentice to Genius.* "[Wright] briskly emerged from his office . . . sat down at the table set with the plot plan and started to draw. . . . The design just poured out of him. Pencils being used up as fast as we could sharpen them. . . . Erasures, overdrawing, modifying. Flipping sheets back and forth. Then, the bold title across the bottom, 'Fallingwater.' A house has to have a name."[3] When Kaufmann walked in, the plans were ready. Kaufmann loved them. He was surprised by one thing though: the waterfall.

In Harmony with Nature

From the beginning, Kaufmann knew the waterfall would be part of his new home. He had pictured the house facing the falls so that the family could look at them every day. Wright, however, worried that if people could see the waterfalls so easily, they would stop looking. The falls would become commonplace and lose their magic. He told Kaufmann, "I want you to live with the waterfall, not just look at it, but for it to become an integral part of your lives."[4]

Kaufmann was enchanted with the idea. When Fallingwater was finally finished, the waterfall could be heard from anywhere in the house—but it could not be seen.

At last, Fallingwater was ready to get off the paper and under construction. It was time to create a masterpiece.

The trees of the highlands give the home a natural frame.

The corner-turning windows (top) and textured rock floors bring nature inside. The ceilings vary from 6 feet to 9 feet high. In some places, tall visitors have to duck.

CHAPTER 4

Welcome to the Cave

Stepping inside Fallingwater is like walking into a cave in the middle of a forest. That is just what Wright intended. The entire place is made of concrete, rock, steel, glass, and sandstone from a nearby quarry. A boulder found on the site was added to the layout of the house. It runs through the living room and doubles as a fireplace hearth. Other beams were bent to go around the trunks of trees, rather than remove the trees.

The walls are made of sandstone, while the floors are polished stone to look as if the river had just rushed through a few minutes before. Barry Bergdoll, professor of art history and archeology at Columbia University, says, "It's as though [Wright] took his inspiration from the ledges that the water is falling over and tried to echo them in the house."[1]

Wright was known for designs with low ceilings. At Fallingwater, anyone over six feet tall has to duck. This adds to the feeling of being inside a cave, surrounded by trees, and serenaded by the waterfall just out of sight. Wright believed this would help people keep their focus outside.

Even the windows in this home support the cave feeling. They are huge, and are "corner turning" windows, meaning they have no frames at the corners. Many of the windows open outward, providing a full view of the forest. (They were also designed without screens. That changed quickly when the Kaufmanns stayed the first summer and mosquitoes joined them inside the house.) Robert McCarter, author of

Chapter 4

Fallingwater: Frank Lloyd Wright, wrote, " . . . the flow of space and movement inside and outside the floors and terraces, gives the house a sense of refuge, while the views and sunlight are framed by steel windows . . ."[2] Skylights in the ceiling let in the natural light and allow for more views of the canopy of trees overhead. Franklin Toker, author of *Fallingwater Rising*, added, "You've never seen a building that fits with nature so tightly. It's not merely nature, it's animated . . . in constant motion."[3]

One of the most startling parts of Fallingwater is a glass hatchway that opens to reveal a staircase. Waiting at the bottom is a 53-inch-deep plunge pool. You can wade in the cool, clear water—or grab a fishing pole. Stephen Atkinson, a California architect who visited Fallingwater, said, "But the *coup de grace* that just melts every architect's heart is this little stair that comes down from the living room.

While the waterfall can be heard from anywhere in the house, the best place to get near it are the stairs down to the water's edge.

Welcome to the Cave

You open this crazy hatch and you can walk downstairs just to the very surface of the water."[4]

Fallingwater, from the first, was built to be a summer home. "It was designed primarily as a weekend retreat, where the Kaufmanns could get a quick fix of nature," says Lynda Waggoner, director of the Fallingwater site. "The house was meant for quiet reflection. The Kaufmanns wanted it to be a total sensory experience." She adds, "There's a blurring between the man-made and what's part of creation. Anyone who says they couldn't live here has to not love nature."[5]

Even the paint used on the house was chosen to blend with nature. Only two colors were chosen. Light ochre, a brownish yellow color, was used on the concrete. Cherokee red was applied to the steel.

In addition to the home, Wright also designed most of its furniture and artwork. Many pieces, including tables and counters, were built into the house itself so that they could never be replaced. The home has several bedrooms, each rather small. One of the oddest aspects are the incredibly low toilets. They are only 10½ inches above the floor;

The colors and textures of the woodwork and furnishings blend with the natural wood and rock of the home.

Chapter 4

most modern toilets are 15 inches high. (This was Kaufmann's idea, not Wright's.)

As stunning as Fallingwater is on the inside, it is the exterior that makes the home so unusual. Almost half of the home's square footage is on the terraces outside. Each of the three stories has a large terrace that stretches out over the falls. From afar, it looks as if the house is floating over the water.

In 1955, Wright told his students at Taliesin, "Fallingwater is a great blessing—one of the great blessings to be experienced here on earth. I think nothing yet ever equaled the coordination . . . of the great principle of repose where forest and stream and rock and all the elements of structure are combined so quietly that really you listen not to any noise whatsoever although the music of the stream is there. But you listen to Fallingwater the way you listen to the quiet of the country."[6]

For Wright, Fallingwater was his comeback to the architectural world. He went on to design many other buildings after Fallingwater, including the Monona Terrace Civic Center in Madison, Wisconsin, and the Guggenheim Museum in New York City.

In January 1938, a few months after Fallingwater was completed, *Time* magazine featured it on the cover, calling it Wright's "most beautiful job." That same year, a guesthouse was added to the property above the main house.

The Kaufmanns were thrilled with their new summer home, even though what was supposed to cost between $20,000 and $30,000 ended up costing $155,0000 (approximately $2.7 million today). Fallingwater was a masterpiece—but it still had a few flaws.

The height of the ceilings in Fallingwater were based on Frank Lloyd Wright's own height. This means that the ceilings vary from just over 9 feet all the way down to 6 feet.

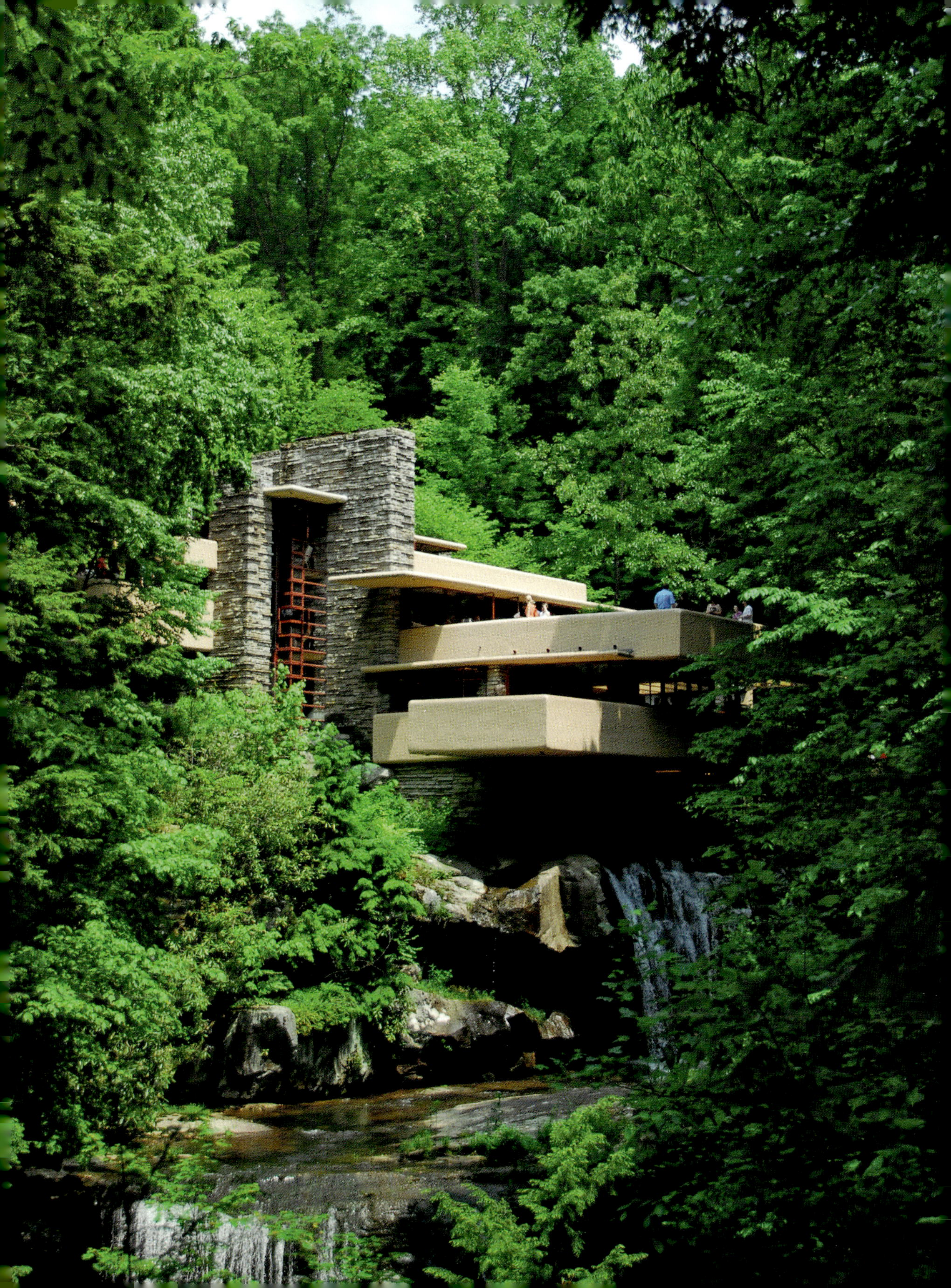

The beauty of the home draws around 160,000 visitors each year. The cost of admission helps cover the cost of keeping the home safe and beautiful.

CHAPTER 5

A Few Flaws

Fallingwater was amazing—but it was not without problems. Skylights leaked, earning the home the nickname of Rising Mildew. The terraces sagged immediately, despite the extra steel reinforcements and supporting walls the contractor added. Some referred to the home as America's Leaning Tower of Pisa.

Despite these issues, the Kaufmanns enjoyed living there for years. After they died, Edgar Kaufmann Jr. inherited the house. In return, in 1963, he donated it to the Western Pennsylvania Conservancy. During the dedication ceremony, he stated:

> [Fallingwater's] beauty remains fresh like that of the nature into which it fits. . . .
>
> House and site together form the very image of man's desire to be at one with nature, equal and wedded to nature. . . .
>
> Fallingwater was created by Frank Lloyd Wright as a declaration that in nature man finds his spiritual as well as his physical energies, that a harmonious response to nature yields the poetry and joy that nourish human living. . . .
>
> The union of powerful art and powerful nature into something beyond the sum of their separate powers deserves to be kept living. . . . I believe the Conservancy will give nature, the source, full due; and art, the human response to nature, full respect.[1]

Chapter 5

The terraces seem to float above the water. In reality, their weight was causing them to sag.

In 1964, Fallingwater was made into a museum so that people could see Wright's work. In 1966, the home was declared a National Historic Landmark.

The Conservancy quickly discovered that the house needed major repair work if it was to keep standing. Over the years, the heavy terraces had continued to sink, sag, and crack.

In 1981, the Conservancy replaced the original roofs and glass on the property. From 2001 to 2009, they made $11.5 million worth of major repairs on the home. They moved over 600 slabs of stone out of the house, first taking the time to carefully number and map them so that they could be put back in the same order. Then they added a concrete beam under the living room terrace. Using high-strength steel cables on each side of the heavy beams, they anchored one end in concrete blocks and the other through a hole drilled in the outside wall of the living room. Hydraulic jacks were used to tighten the cables and anchor them.

A Few Flaws

Since Fallingwater became a museum in 1964, more than five million people have come to tour the house. There are lectures and special exhibits offered as well. As in the past, students and artists can still visit for workshops and lessons on architecture. In 1991, the home was named "best all-time work of American architecture" by the American Institute of Architects.

Some celebrities have come to see Fallingwater. In 2006, actor Brad Pitt toured the house and was amazed. Ever since he had taken an architectural history class in college, he had wanted to see Wright's designs up close. Curator Cara Armstrong said, "He and I talked quite a bit about design and art. He was incredibly well-informed about architecture." Following the tour, Pitt celebrated his birthday in the living room. "Brad said he had a visual sense of Fallingwater but experiencing it in person, hearing the sound of the waterfall cascading under the house and smelling the wood from the fireplace, was better than anything he could have imagined."[2]

Wright would have been pleased.

Fallingwater is worth a visit no matter the weather. There are even complementary umbrellas available if it rains. Some tourists have said the rain added to their experience.

Chronology

1867	Frank Lloyd Wright is born in rural Wisconsin.
1885	Edgar J. Kaufmann Sr. is born in Pittsburgh, Pennsylvania.
1910	Edgar J. Kaufmann Jr. is born in Pittsburgh.
1932	Wright publishes his autobiography and establishes Taliesin Fellowship in Wisconsin.
1934	Kaufmann Jr. meets Wright and begins his apprenticeship at Taliesin.
1935	Kaufmann Sr. hires Wright to design a summer home for him.
1936	Construction on Fallingwater begins (April).
1937	Construction is finished (December) and the Kaufmanns move in.
1939	Fallingwater's guesthouse is completed.
1955	Kaufmann Sr. dies.
1959	Wright dies.
1963	Kaufmann Jr. deeds Fallingwater to the Western Pennsylvania Conservancy.
1964	Fallingwater opens for public tours.
1976	Fallingwater is designated as a National Historic Landmark.

Chronology

1989 Kaufmann Jr. dies.

2002–2009 Massive renovations are made to Fallingwater.

2016 Flooding topples several statues at Fallingwater. They are rescued and restored.

2017 Fallingwater hits 5.5 million visitors.

Fallingwater's large windows allow for natural light to brighten the dark wood and stone interior.

Chapter Notes

Chapter 1
1. "Frank Lloyd Wright: Life and Work." PBS, undated.
2. Carpenter, Mackenzie. "Wright's Fallingwater Still Breathtaking at 75." *Pittsburgh Post-Gazette*, November 27, 2011.
3. Ibid.

Chapter 2
1. "Frank Lloyd Wright Biography." Biography.com, undated.
2. "Taliesin Was Frank Lloyd Wright's Estate in the Hills of Wisconsin." Frank Lloyd Wright.org, undated.

Chapter 3
1. "Taliesin Was Frank Lloyd Wright's Estate in the Hills of Wisconsin." Frank Lloyd Wright.org, undated.
2. "Fallingwater." *USA Home and Garden*, undated.
3. Tafel, Edgard. *Years with Frank Lloyd Wright: Apprentice to Genius*. Mineola, NY: Courier Dover Publications, 1979.
4. Jaffe, Eric. "Frank Lloyd Wright's Most Beautiful Work." *Smithsonian*, January 2008.

Chapter 4
1. Hall, Shannon. "Fallingwater: A Building that Bonds with Nature and Dances with Time." *Nautilus*, June 10, 2015.
2. McCarter, Robert. *Fallingwater: Frank Lloyd Wright*. New York: Phaidon, 1994.
3. Jaffe, Eric. "Frank Lloyd Wright's Most Beautiful Work." *Smithsonian*, January 2008.
4. Hall.
5. McKay, Gretchen. "Kentuck Knob Edges Out Fallingwater as More Livable Home." *Pittsburgh Post-Gazette*, June 23, 2001.
6. "Quotes about Fallingwater." Fallingwater.org.
7. Jaffe.

Chapter 5
1. "Quotes about Fallingwater." Fallingwater.org.
2. Associated Press. "Pitt Falls for Lloyd Wright's Fallingwater." *Today*, December 8, 2006.

Further Reading

Books

Armstrong, Cara. *Moxie: The Dachshund of Fallingwater.* Houston, TX: Bright Sky Press, 2010.

Harshman, Marc, and Anna Egan Smucker. *Fallingwater: The Building of Frank Lloyd Wright's Masterpiece.* New York: Roaring Brook Press, 2017.

Labrecque, Ellen, and Who HQ. *Who Was Frank Lloyd Wright?* London: Penguin Workshop, 2015.

Mudpuppy. *I Heart Architecture with Frank Lloyd Wright.* New York: Mudpuppy Press, 2017.

Thorne-Thomsen, Kathleen. *Frank Lloyd Wright for Kids: His Life and Ideas.* Chicago: Chicago Review Press, 2014.

Works Consulted

Associated Press. "Pitt Falls for Lloyd Wright's Fallingwater." *Today*, December 8, 2006. http://www.today.com/id/16113827/ns/today-today_entertainment/t/pitt-falls-lloyd-wrights-fallingwater/#.We-ux1tSzb0

Carpenter, Mackenzie. "Wright's Fallingwater Still Breathtaking at 75." *Pittsburgh Post-Gazette,* November 27, 2011. http://www.post-gazette.com/ae/art-architecture/2011/11/27/Wright-s-Fallingwater-still-breathtaking-at-75/stories/201111270232

Fallingwater. https:www.fallingwater.org

"Fallingwater." *USA Home and Garden*, undated. http://usahomeandgarden.com/architecture/fallingwater/fallingwater.html

"Frank Lloyd Wright Biography." Biography.com, undated. https://www.biography.com/people/frank-lloyd-wright-9537511

Frank Lloyd Wright.org. http://franklloydwright.org/taliesin/

"Frank Lloyd Wright: Life and Work." PBS, undated. http://www.pbs.org/flw/buildings/index.html

Further Reading

Hall, Shannon. "Fallingwater: A Building that Bonds with Nature and Dances with Time." *Nautilus*, June 10, 2015. http://nautil.us/blog/fallingwater-a-building-that-bonds-with-nature-and-dances-with-time

Jaffe, Eric. "Frank Lloyd Wright's Most Beautiful Work." *Smithsonian*, January 2008. https://www.smithsonianmag.com/travel/frank-lloyd-wrights-most-beautiful-work-12103484/

McCarter, Robert. *Fallingwater: Frank Lloyd Wright*. New York: Phaidon, 1994.

McKay, Gretchen. "Kentuck Knob Edges Out Fallingwater as More Livable Home." *Pittsburgh Post-Gazette*, June 23, 2001. http://old.post-gazette.com/homes/20010623wright0623fnp3.asp

Tafel, Edgard. *Years with Frank Lloyd Wright: Apprentice to Genius*. Mineola, NY: Courier Dover Publications, 1979. https://www.khanacademy.org/humanities/ap-art-history/later-europe-and-americas/modernity-ap/a/frank-lloyd-wright-fallingwater

On the Internet

Fallingwater: Live Camera
   https://www.fallingwater.org/fallingwater-cam/

Frank Lloyd Wright Foundation: "The Life of Frank Lloyd Wright"
   http://franklloydwright.org/frank-lloyd-wright/

Frank Lloyd Wright's Fallingwater
   http://www.wright-house.com/frank-lloyd-wright/fallingwater-pictures/pictures-of-fallingwater.html

Frank Lloyd Wright's Taliesin
   http://www.taliesinpreservation.org/

Glossary

architect (AR-kih-tekt)—A person who designs buildings.

blueprint (BLOO-print)—A drawing that shows how to build something.

cantilever (KAN-tih-lee-ver)—A beam or support that is anchored only at one end.

conservancy (kun-SER-vun-see)—An organization focused on saving things such as historical sites or wildlife.

coup de grace (KOO deh GRAHS)—The final, decisive thing or event.

curator (KYUR-ay-tur)—The keeper of a museum.

hearth (HARTH)—The brick or stone floor of a fireplace.

hydraulic (hy-DRAH-lik)—Moved or operated by the pressure in a liquid (such as water or oil).

integral (in-TEG-rul)—Necessary to make something complete or whole.

mildew (MIL-doo)—A usually white fungus that grows in damp places.

ochre (OH-kur)—A pale brownish yellow color.

quarry (KWAR-ee)—A large, deep pit from which stones or other materials are taken.

repose (ree-POHZ)—To rest in a particular place.

sensory (SEN-sor-ee)—Something experienced through the ears, eyes, mouth, nose, or skin.

terrace (TAYR-is)—A flat area next to a building that is usually used for sitting or eating; a porch or patio.

tributary (TRIH-byoo-tayr-ee)—A river or stream that flows into a larger river or lake.

PHOTO CREDITS: Cover—Olkinderhook; Back cover—Bill Simon; p. 1—Jason Shenk; p. 4—Shinya Suzuki, Mechanismo; pp. 4, 6, 7, 8, 14—Public Domain; p. 8—Raunaq Gupta; p. 10—IIP Photo Archive; p. 11—My Lil Rotten; pp. 12, 13—SK; p. 14—Sikeri; pp. 16, 19—Lykantrop; p. 18—Daderot, p. 21—Bill Simpson; p. 22—R London; p. 24—ruhrfisch; p. 25—Paul Simpson; p. 27—Jeremy Weate. Every measure has been taken to find all copyright holders of material used in this book. In the event any mistakes or omissions have happened within, attempts to correct them will be made in future editions of the book.

Index

American Institute of Architects 25

Armstrong, Cara 25

Atkinson, Stephen 18–19

Bear Run Tributary 10

Bergdoll, Barry 17

Carnegie Science Center 8

Fallingwater
  cantilevers 4, 5, 13
  cost 7, 20, 24
  furnishings 13, 16, 17, 19
  guesthouse 20
  as museum 24–25
  National Historic Landmark 24
  plans 6–7, 14
  restoration 22, 24
  stairs 18–19
  terraces 5, 18, 20, 23, 24
  Visitors Center 12
  waterfall 5, 13, 14–15, 17, 18, 20, 25
  windows 17, 18

Fallingwater: Frank Lloyd Wright 17–18

Fallingwater: Rising 18

Guggenheim Museum 20

Hall, Walter 5

Kaufmann, Edgar J., Jr. 11, 17, 19, 23

Kaufmann, Edgar J., Sr. 5–7, 9–10, 11, 13, 14–15, 17, 19, 20, 23

Laurel Highlands 12

McCarter, Robert 17–18

Monona Terrace Civic Center 20

Pitt, Brad 25

Pittsburgh 7, 8, 9

Taffel, Edgar 14

Taliesin Art School 10–11, 20

Toker, Franklin 18

Waggoner, Lynda 19

Western Pennsylvania Conservancy 23, 24

Wright, Frank Lloyd 5–7, 9–10, 11, 13, 14, 15, 17, 20. 23, 24, 25

Years with Frank Lloyd Wright: Apprentice to Genius 14